Praise for HARMONYVILLE

"Jon is one of the warmest, funniest, freest, most musical people I know. And all of that is in his book. It is loaded with groan-worthy puns and extended riffs (and extended dominants) on the subject that is dear to his heart and mine: harmony. The personalities he ascribes to notes and chords are hilarious and approachable. Oops, I mean 'relatable.' After you read Jon's book, you will never again be able to say, 'Oh that stuff is all math, I can't understand it.'"
—JOE MULHOLLAND
CHAIR EMERITUS, HARMONY DEPARTMENT, BERKLEE COLLEGE OF MUSIC

"With *Harmonyville 01625* Jon welcomes us all in and gives us the opportunity to explore and venture further into the wonderful world of his imagination."
—BILL FRISELL
GRAMMY-WINNING GUITARIST

"*Welcome to Harmonyville* is a fun ride through the trials and tribulations of two chord symbols that have come to life. Mr. Damian's creativity is boundless, and not limited to the fretboard!"
—JAMES VALENTINE, MAROON 5
GRAMMY-WINNING GUITARIST

"One of the great musical innovations of all time seems obvious to us now—harmony. Jon Damian's book creates a fun and educational way of understanding harmony, a simple concept with myriad applications that has provided us so many musical riches."
—ROGER H. BROWN
PRESIDENT, BERKLEE COLLEGE OF MUSIC

Also by Jon Damian

THE GUITARIST'S GUIDE TO COMPOSING AND IMPROVISING

• • •

THE CHORD FACTORY: BUILD YOUR OWN GUITAR CHORD DICTIONARY

• • •

FRESH MUSIC: EXPLORATIONS WITH THE CREATIVE WORKSHOP ENSEMBLE FOR MUSICIANS, ARTISTS, AND TEACHERS

MAP of HARMONYVILLE

Praise for JON DAMIAN

"….a very special musician"
—MIKE STERN

"….and the rhythm guitar part was handled beautifully by Jon Damian"
—KEITH LOCKHART
BOSTON POPS CONDUCTOR

"…the most experienced and admired guitar teacher I know."
—JIM HALL
LEGENDARY GUITARIST
AND NEA JAZZ MASTERS FELLOW

"That guy is out!"
—JIMMY GIUFFRE
A LEGEND IN JAZZ

"I received the most valuable elements from Jon's Creative Workshop, opening a door of endless creativity in me as a film composer and concert artist."
STEPHANE WREMBEL
COMPOSER OF "BISTRO FADA,"
THE THEME FOR WOODY ALLEN'S
MIDNIGHT IN PARIS

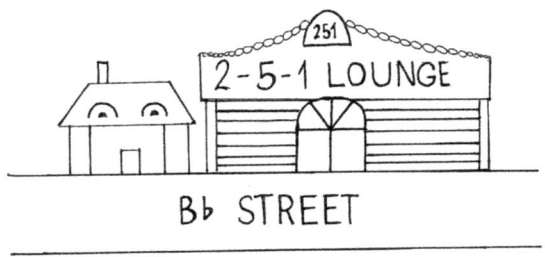

© 2021 by Jon Damian. All rights reserved.

No part of this book may be reproduced or transmitted in any form or by any means, electronic or mechanical including photocopying, recording, or by any information storage and retrieval system (beyond that copying permitted by Section 107 and 108 of the U.S. Copyright Law and except by reviewers for the public press) without written permission from the publishers.

Welcome to Harmonyville 01625

An original story written and illustrated and published by Jon Damian

YO! Publications
11 Alpine Street
Cambridge, MA 02138
jongennarodamian@gmail.com

ISBN 987-0-578-96152-1

Editing: Betsy Damian
Cover Art: Jon Damian
Book Design: Kathy Kikkert
Copy Editor: Steve Korn

PRINTED IN THE UNITED STATES OF AMERICA

Welcome to Harmonyville 01625 is a work of fiction. All the characters, except for Jon, are music chord symbols infused with life. Any resemblance of characters to any actual people could easily be taken.

I dedicate this book to my loving family, friends, my saints and angels, and to all who put up with my bad jokes.

CONTENTS

Foreword by Bill Frisell • 11

Preface • 13

Cast in Order of Appearance • 15

Map of Harmonyville • 16

Introduction • 19

Our Story Begins • 24

The Harmonyville Times Chord Symbols Crosstones Puzzle • 36

The Dominante Family Compound • 41

The Chord Academy Awards • 54

Harmonic Equality Scenario • 63

Epilogue • 125

A Smidge More • 132

Epilogue Plus • 134

The Puzzle Answers • 137

Glossarium • 138

A Brief History • 145

Acknowledgements • 148

FOREWORD
by Bill Frisell

I met Jon Damian in 1975. He became my teacher then and is my teacher now. Forty six years!! Wow. He came along at just the right moment. I was stuck. He broke the doors open. Helped me to see things from a different angle. Possibilities. He's still doing that. It keeps going to this day. With *Harmonyville 01625,* Jon welcomes us all in and gives us the opportunity to explore and venture further into the wonderful world of his imagination. Remember when you were a real little kid and curious? When you'd see something for the very first time and be surprised and amazed by it? How your mind would be blown? I don't ever want to forget. Jon reminds us how to stay in touch with that feeling. This stuff is important.
Thank you, Jon.

Bill Frisell

PREFACE

Hello. My name is Jon Damian, author of this harmonic tome, *Welcome to Harmonyville 01625*. I have always loved harmony, the world of chords, and chord symbol language. This love was kindled while listening to my sister Judy's wonderful record collection. As a 3 year old, I was immersed in great jazz bands and singers from Ella to Frank, whose terrific bands accompanied them with arrangements filled with wonderful harmonic and rhythmic ideas. Next, I discovered my first guitar hero, Tony Mottola, on *The Tonight Show Starring Johnny Carson* and I was thrilled when I'd watch Tony step out as a featured soloist. Tony inspired me to teach myself to play guitar. In high school, I began to sing in a cappella groups on the street corners of Brooklyn, and down in its reverb-filled subway stations. The music consisted mainly of simple harmonies which always sounded and felt wonderful. When I was singing, I loved how my whole body would vibrate sympathetically with the sound. So now I offer *Welcome to Harmonyville 01625,* which brings those fascinating chord symbols to life in the form of harmonic characters acting out a comedic play through various scenes. Hey! Break a root! If you got that bad pun, you're warmed up for a fun time. Welcome to town!!! What's a root? Just keep reading!

P.S. While having fun exploring Harmonyville, you may wish to visit The Glossarium, a dome-shaped structure in North Harmonyville, that is a library with definitions for musical terms you will come across. Enter The Glossarium on page 138.

CAST
in Order of Appearance

Jon	Minor Dee	Sharpie
Ms. La Majeur	Dimbee	Dr. Mi So
Guido B. Dominante	Auntie B	B Lama Monad
Jim-E	General Dominante	Affy Bemolle
Gino Dominante	Maestro Mejor	Dr. La Haupt
Bb Bobby Straight	Ray Bemolle	Reverend A. Sharpe
Fi-Do	C Jam	Chester
Dee Mineur Septième	Eddie Flat	Baby Cadenza
Baby Amy	Cousin Nicky	XYLA
Emmy Lou	David Dyad	Juliette
Mama C	Triton	Romeo
Uncle Fa	Augie Tonale	Ratunda

MAP of HARMONYVILLE

Just to get our bearings, here is a **MAP** of Harmonyville. This map will guide visitors through the streets and scenes of Harmonyville.

EACH SCENE HAS MAP COORDINATES inside a compass indicating a letter on the map's left and a number on the map's bottom. For example: in the Leaning Tower of Pizza Scene is the compass with coordinates D6. Connecting these coordinates will take you to 300 Bb Street. It's fun to follow the locations as the scenes unfold. For out-of-town locations, the coordinates will bring you to a sign directing you to that location.

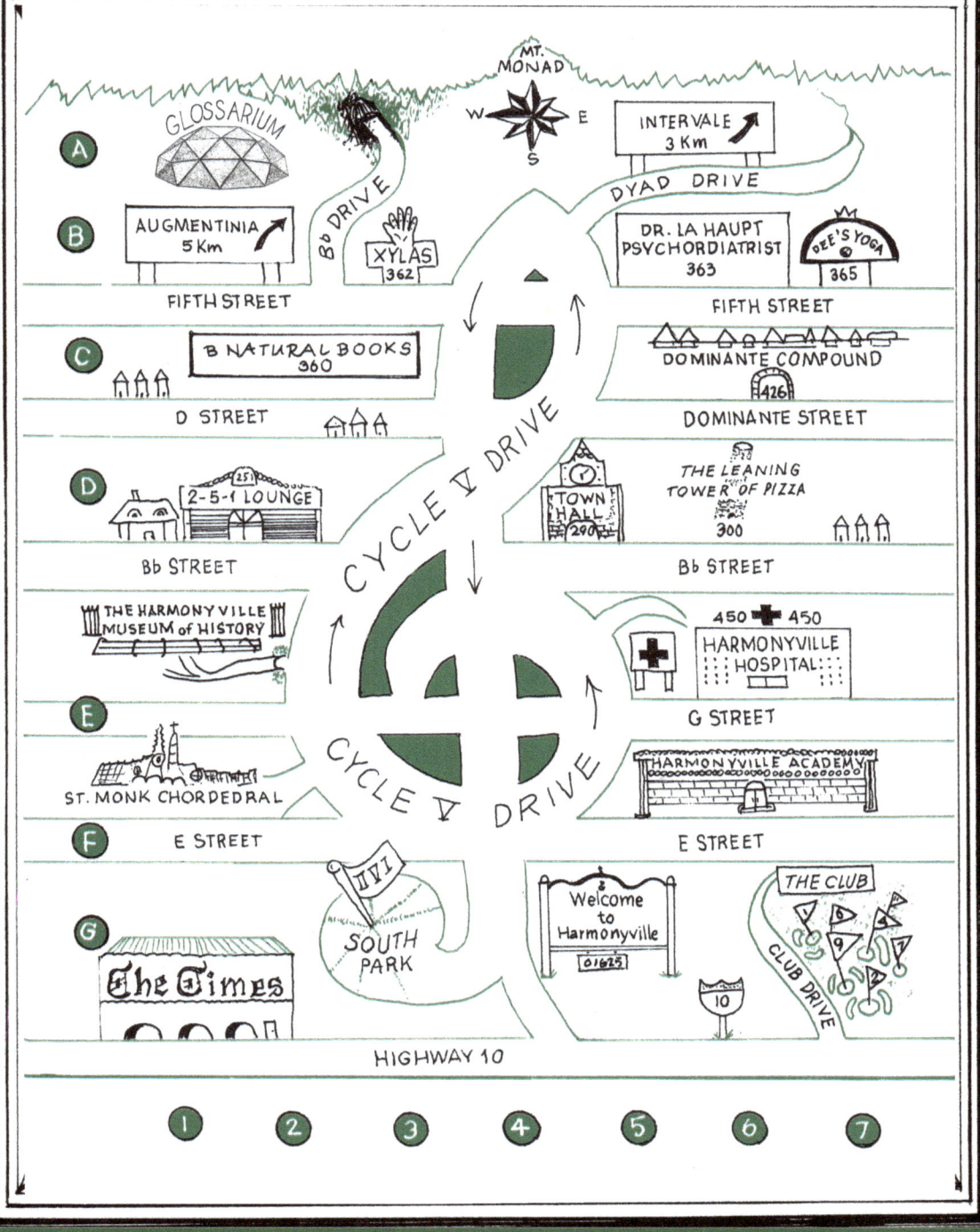

The Leaning Tower's
Jackson Pollock Pizza

HARMONYVILLE

is a small town whose population consists of chord symbols infused with life through illustrations and narrative. Our main characters are Gino Dominante, a portly G7 chord symbol, and his subdominant other, Dee Mineur Septiéme, is a petite D Minor 7 chord symbol. In the world of music, a chord symbol is a form of notation that uses letters and numbers to indicate a particular chord. Each chord symbol has a unique personality. Some sound beautiful, some are mild-mannered, some are aggressive, and some are just middle-of-the-road kinds of characters. Like homo sapiens (that's us humans), chord symbols live in families. Just for fun, let's think of chord symbols as Harmono Sapiens! The inter-relationships between chord symbols, as between humans, can be harmonious or not harmonious. Harmony consists of a series of notes, piled vertically (I think of it like the vertebrae of a human skeleton).

For fun, I made Harmonyville's ZIP code 01625 since it indicates the roots or bottom notes of the chords of an oft-used progression of chords; a 1 6 2 5 progression. Hundreds of popular tunes use it as a harmonic foundation to build their melodies on, for example, "Blue Moon."

Here is what the chord symbols of a 1 6 2 5 chord progression look like in the key of C. Note that a dash signifies a minor chord (for example, A– is an A minor chord).   C A– D– G7

To hear some nice chords, or harmonies, just do a Web search for the Doo Wop groups from the 1950s and the '60s, Barbershop Quartets and recent boy bands. I can hear this boy band warming up! …

As with all relationships, our main characters, Gino and Dee have their ups and downs. They're joined by a line-up of zany characters; from a monad (a one-note chord), to an X Major triad (one of my made-up three-note chords!).

Now, let's meet my alter-ego in Harmonyville, who will guide us in our adventures around town.

JON: I am not originally from Harmonyville. As a cartoonist and reporter for Harmonyville's newspaper, <u>The Harmonyville Times</u>, I do the MAC+DC series for the paper. Gino Dominante and I have become good friends since I starting writing this book. Follow me as your intrepid narrator throughout this journey. I love working on my trusty Olivetti Letera typewriter.

I will use <u>play tags</u> for ease of communication.

Here is an example just to get you warmed up.

JON: Greetings, Dear Readers!

YOU: Hi, Jon.

JON: You catch on fast!

YOU: Thanks.

JON: It's a lot easier than using Morse code!

YOU: I don't know Morse code.

JON: Exactly! Just for kicks translate this Morse code message.

(just do a Web search for Morse code.)

Now that we have our bearings, we can begin our story at The Harmonyville Museum of History. You can find it on the map, right off of Cycle Five Drive. Let's check out a class lecture by Ms. La Majeur, a lovely A Major Triad.

OUR STORY BEGINS

MS. LA: Good morning, class. Today, I will speak about our town's history and ancestry. Then we will look at an incredible diorama that shows the harmonic evolution of an E7#9 chord. Harmonyville was founded in 1870 by B Lama Monad, a one-note chord who lives atop Mt. Monad. Some folks think B Lama to be close to 200 years old. His chanting is thought to have curative powers.

A STUDENT: Ms. La, can we visit B Lama Monad?

MS. LA: Yes. You must hire a guide from Intervale named David Dyad, a power chord. Mt. Monad's base straddles three towns, primarily Intervale, and small areas in Augmentinia and Harmonyville. You can find Mt. Monad on the map due north of town. Harmonyville's name is inspired by a town called Armonia in Italy, which was the original home of many of our town elders. Here in this display case is a lovely postcard of Armonia in 1922. It is a 70th birthday greeting to Guido B. Dominante.

CARTOLINA POSTALE ITALIANA

Agosto 20, 1922

Ciao Guido!

Buon settantesimo
compleanno!
Molti Abbracci
Maria Adagio

A GUIDO DOMINANTE
426 D. STREET
HARMONYVILLE 01625
USA

ARMONIA ITALIA 1922

MS. LA: Here is a portrait of Guido painted by an unknown artist from Armonia. He is Gino Dominante's Great, Great, Great, Great, Great, Grandfather. He is the first G Major Triad to arrive in Harmonyville in 1875.

And this is Fort Degree, which was destroyed in the Augmentinian Crisis. The Glossarium was built on the Fort's site in the foothills of Mt. Monad.

MS. LA: Now, please follow me to the Hall of Evolution to see the diorama.

STUDENTS: Wow! Super! Who made that?

MS. LA: This diorama was made by a mystic named XYLA, an X Major chord who can see into the future, as well as deeply into the past. She built these sculptures from a vision she had in her crystal ball.

STUDENTS: Coooooolll!! Can we visit XYLA?

MS. LA: Visiting her is expensive. Her studio is on Fifth and Bb Drive.

JON: Thanks, Ms. La, for letting us listen to your lecture.

MS. LA: It is a pleasure, sir.

JON: Now, let's see who is coming down Bb Street!

WELCOME TO HARMONYVILLE. I AM GINO, A DOMINANT V7 CHORD. I HAVE AN A TYPE PERSONALITY. HEY! WAD'YA EXPECT?!

JON: Look, here comes Gino's best friend!

GINO: Hey Bobby!

Bb BOBBY STRAIGHT: Hey Gino! Come on in!

JON: The next morning, Bb Bobby gives Gino a call. Shhhh....let's listen in.

JON: Let's see if we can find out more about Dee.

She may be at the 2–5–1 Lounge with Gino.

JON: Dee Mineur Septiéme is a perfect match for Gino, harmonically speaking. Dee is a yogini with her own studio, located on Fifth Street. Dee is a <u>Harmonyville Times Crosstones</u> <u>Puzzle</u> addict as well as an excellent vocalist. Her voice and Gino's bass trombone will make beautiful music together.

GINO: Dee, would you like to come to the Dominante Compound to meet some of my family?

DEE: That sounds great, Gino.

GINO: Here's a little something for you.

DEE: How did you know I love doing the *Times* puzzle!?

GINO: A little birdie tweeted in my ear.

JON: It looks like Gino and Dee are getting along nicely. FYI, this puzzle is fun. I built it originally for my book <u>The Chord Factory: Build Your Own Guitar Chord Dictionary.</u> I used an actual blank grid from <u>The New York Times</u> so I thought it would be a nice fit for <u>The Harmonyville Times</u>. It took me a while to build it. Can you finish it before this 30-minute hourglass runs out?? Time yourself!! Ready. Set. Go!!

The Harmonyville Times
The Chord Symbols Crosstones Puzzle

Dee, I started The Times Puzzle for you. Love, Gina

ACROSS

1	CMaj7(9)
6	F
9	B♭–7
13	D–7(9)
18	E♭Maj7(9)
19	A♭
20	D–7
21	D♭Maj7#5(9,#11)
22	G♭Maj7(9)
23	C–
24	F–Maj7
25	A–7(9)
26	B♭°
27	A°
28	F–
30	G–
31	F#°
33	C–
34	C
35	B–7♭5

38	E♭+	118	G7(9)	55	F#–(First Inversion)
42	G♭	119	G♭Maj7#5	56	A–(First Inversion)
43	D7	120	E♭	60	E
44	G	122	FMaj7(9)	61	G
45	C7	124	B♭7(9, #11)	62	B°
49	F#–7♭5	125	B♭7	63	D
50	B°7	126	G	65	C–
52	E♭Maj7	127	AMaj7(9)	66	G–
53	D7	128	DMaj7(9)	68	F–
57	A–	129	D♭Maj7#5	69	A–
58	B♭+	130	B♭	70	C–
59	C7♭5(♭9)	131	C7(9)	71	G–Maj7
61	G7(9, #11, 13)			72	G♭+
64	C#–7♭5	**DOWN**		73	B♭
65	C7#5	1	C–7♭5	74	D♭
66	GMaj7	2	E°7	76	E♭–7
67	D	3	G°7	78	G♭Maj7(9)
68	F7	4	B°	79	B♭7(♭9)
71	G–7(9)	5	D°	80	D♭Maj7(9)
72	G♭	6	F–Maj7	82	A♭+
75	A♭Maj7	7	A°	83	C
76	E♭–Maj7	8	C–7(9)	84	E♭
77	E♭–7	9	B♭Maj7(9)	85	A♭Maj7
81	B♭7(9, #11, 13)	10	D♭Maj7(9)	86	C7(9)
83	C°	11	F7(9)	89	A–(First Inversion)
85	A♭+	12	A♭+	91	A–
87	B♭	13	D–7(9)	92	B♭–Maj7
88	D–7♭5	14	F–	93	B♭Maj7
89	C7	15	A–7	99	F–
90	F#–7♭5	16	C–7	103	D7(9)
92	B♭–7	17	E–7	104	E♭Maj7(9)
94	E°7	29	A♭Maj7	105	G–7(9)
95	C–	31	F#–7♭5	106	B♭7(9)
96	D♭Maj7	32	C–Maj7(9)	107	A♭Maj7(9)
97	G♭	35	B–7(9)	109	E♭Maj7
98	D–	36	D7(9)	110	GMaj7
100	E°	37	FMaj7(9)	111	B–7♭5
101	F–7♭5	39	GMaj7	114	G♭Maj7#5
102	B°7	40	B°	115	A♭Maj7#5
104	E♭	41	G–	116	C7#5
108	D–	45	C–7♭5	117	E♭Maj7#5
109	E♭+	46	E°	119	G♭
112	F#°	47	G–	121	G
113	G–	48	B♭	122	F
115	A♭	51	A♭+	123	A
		54	D (First Inversion)		

You will find the solutions to the puzzle, if you wish, on page 137.

JON: I have found that the puzzle helps make learning music theory fun as does writing this book; breathing life into chord symbols. At this point, after many hours of illustrating my characters in various settings, I feel that they are really alive!

DEE: I also love the MAC+DC cartoons on the back page of the *Times*. It is like a tonic for my spirits. Here take a look!

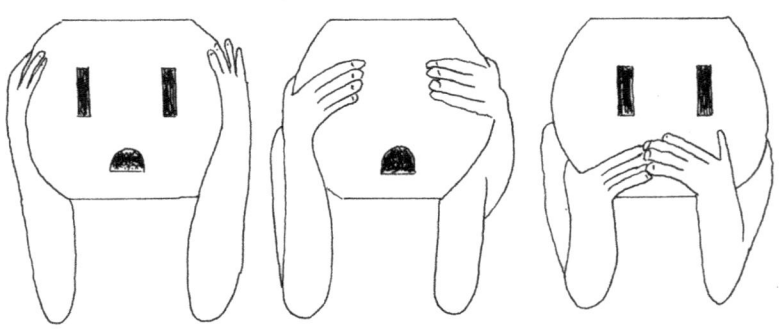

MAC+DC by Jon

GINO: Welcome, Dee, to the Dominante Compound. The Dominante family has been living here for decades, since shortly after Harmonyville's founding in 1870. Say, a big birthday is coming up for our town soon. Our family history began in Armonia, Italy, a beautiful town. I hope to visit Armonia someday. I am aways hearing wonderful stories about it.

DEE: Thanks for inviting me to the compound. Wow! What a beautiful group of people in this photo!

GINO: That's some of the Dominantes.

JON: Gino, may I let Dee know who's who in this lovely family portrait? Quite a cast of zany characters, as you may have noticed already.

GINO: Thanks, Jon.

JON: From the left is Gino, baby Amy and Emmy Lou on Mama C's knees, Uncle Fa with Minor Dee, Dimbee and Auntie B. Below is General Dominante, Gino's grandfather, who died in the Augmentinian Conflict, a sad affair. What a set of medals!

DEE: And who is this sweet baby here?

GINO: Oh, that's me on Mama C's lap.

DEE: You were the cutest!!

GINO: I remember Mama calling me "my little meatball" as she tweaked my cheeks! Speaking of meatballs, wait until you try her wonderful cooking. She's always wanted to have her own ristorante. Every Sunday she makes a full meal from the antipasto to the dolci. Do you have any pictures?

DEE: I have a few at my home that I hope to show you along with my "special collection" when you visit.

GINO: Your "special collection" intrigues me.

DEE: I may have a photo in my bag. I have to dig a little....Ahhh. Here it is. Speaking of moms, my mother used to kid me about my overstuffed handbag. She would say, "Dee, you could grow potatoes in that bag!!

GINO: Your mom sounds very sweet. The acorn falls not far from the tree.

DEE: Nice family photos, Gino. Here is one of me as a happy child. It brings me nice memories! This photo was taken on my 6th birthday at South Park. It was my first of many happy moments at the park. And I'm sure many more to come!

GINO: How sweet you were with your jump-rope, Dee. And I bet with great time! Brava! What a beautiful photo. And what a nice handbag!

DEE: Gino, you can come by my pad on D Street, 3rd house in from Cycle V Drive and see my bag collection sometime!

GINO: Sounds great, Dee. So that's what you meant by your "special collection."

JON: Speaking of cute children, let's first check out what some of the younger of the Dominantes are up to. Let's take a quick visit with Gino over to Dee's pad on D Street.

DEE: Gino, thanks for dropping by. So, here's part of my handbag collection. I love the way some of the bags take on a facial characteristic especially the bottom two rows. I actually have names for each of them. Sorry, I don't mean to bore you.

GINO: I am simply enchanted by all this beauty! **WOOOOOOW!!** You have great taste in fashion.

DEE: And in men too!

GINO: Aw–jee-whizz!

DEE: Speaking of collections, I save all the MAC+DC cartoons. Here are Jon's first two MAC+DC cartoons from when he started working for *The Harmonyville Times*.

GINO: Thanks for showing me! I get a kick out of them!

JON: Now let's check out the younger Dominantes in action. As you can see Amy is a sweetheart. Bb Bobby Straight is a cool uncle and does some great barbecue!

JON: And here is her brother Dimbee showing some support for Uncle Fa.

JON: Here's another brother, Minor Dee, on the way to his guitar lesson at the Academy.

JON: Now, a more distant relative arrives. Gino's cousin is visiting from Armonia, Italy. He is a Db chord. Hence his name Ray Bemolle. In Italian, Bemolle means flat.

JON: He plays clarinet. He is quickly picking up town slang........ harmie! And gigs!

THE CHORD ACADEMY AWARDS

Since the Academy of Motion Picture Arts and Sciences awards an Oscar for the Best Movie at the Academy Awards, why not have a group of musicians act as the Harmonyville Academy and cast their vote for the Hardest Working Chord Symbol?

I used a popular social media platform and sent out a request to my friends. Which chord symbol has worked the hardest for you?

A good number of votes came back.

Who won the Harmonyville Academy Award? Over the next few scenes you will find out!

Make a guess.

JON: Here is Gino and Dee's Band, The Turnarounds, crossing Cycle V Drive, Harmonyville's main street. C Jam on trumpet, Eddie Flat on guitar, Dee Mineur on vocals and Gino on bass trombone.

JON: Let's sing along with Dee and the Turnarounds. She's put lyrics to the melody of "Chattanooga Choo Choo." The crowd seems to be enjoying themselves.

MAESTRO MEJOR: On behalf of Harmonyville Academy, I present you the Chord Academy Award for the Hardest Working Chord Symbol for 2020.

JON: You may have noticed that The Turnarounds' new guitarist Eddie Flat didn't get much attention at the awards gig. Let's remedy that.

HI. I'M EDDIE FLAT. I AM THE NEW GUITARIST WITH THE TURNAROUNDS. I JUST PLAYED MY FIRST GIG WITH THEM AT THE ACADEMY CHORD AWARDS. IT WAS OK, BUT I WOULD RATHER BE PLAYING SOLO GIGS. THEN I'D NEVER BE LATE FOR REHEARSALS! HOPE TO SEE YOU AT MY SOLO GIG AT GINO'S PARTY.

JON: Bb Bobby Straight is showing off his barbecue chops at the family party for Gino! YUM!

JON: Sorry, I let my ego jump into this scene. I just had to do it! My last name is Damian. I just put an accent over the second "a" in Damian. Voilá... Damián! As you remember, when Gino first visited Dee's pad there were 20 of her designer handbags! Something like Imelda Marcos' shoes!! Imelda was a Filipino politician, and was the First Lady of the Philippines for 21 years. She and her husband notoriously spent other people's money. Imelda had a collection of 888 handbags, 1000 pairs of shoes and 500 mink coats!!

GINO: I found this beauty for Dee in a little shop in Intervale for our one-and-a-half month significant other anniversary. This bag is an actual Imelda Marcos bag. Dee will love it. I hope so, it wasn't cheap!

HARMONIC EQUALITY SCENARIO

In humankind, in general, there are always disputes about who is more special. This leads to judgments of inequality. Here, in Harmonyville, home to chords consisting generally of three or more notes, there is a population of residents who feel that harmonic structures consisting of less than that to be inferior, and not to be considered as legitimate harmonies. Thankfully, there is a group of harmonic activists, led by Jim-E, trying to change this attitude and make all-sized harmonies from monads (one-note structures), to extended chords, equal in harmonic stature. Here is an issue of *The Harmonyville Times* that has a front-page feature interview conducted by Harmonyville's Jim-E with Intervale's David Dyad, a Power Chord consisting of a Perfect Fifth, a dyad, or two-note chord. David has a compelling discourse that he wants to deliver to Harmonyville residents. Let's check out the interview and the scenes that follow.

The Harmonyville Times

JIM-E, AWARD-WINNING ACTIVIST, INVITES DAVID DYAD FROM INTERVALE FOR HARMONIC EQUALITY CONFERENCE

Intervale, a neighboring town to Harmonyville is noted for its residents who are primarily two-note structures. Here is an interview Jim-E did with David Dyad.

Activist Jim-E

Power Chord David Dyad

Jim: Welcome to Harmonyville, David.

David: Thanks for the invite.

Jim: Intervale is noted for its population of two-note structures.

David: First, we in Intervale consider ourselves as Dyads; two-note chords with as much harmonic integrity as any sized chord.

Jim: Folks in Harmonyville feel that two-note structures are incomplete; no 3rd.....?

David: If I look incomplete you need your eyes checked! I am a Power Chord, a perfect fifth, as stable as a rock in sound. Harmonyville's population of chord symbols would be out of a job if it wasn't for the solid foundation we provide.

Jim: But only two notes, how...??

David: Listen carefully, less is not least. With Dyads, two-note chords, the timbres, overtones of each note are heard more readily.

Jim: How can I help to convince Harmonyvillians of your succinct points?

David: Jim, I would love to do a lecture at your Academy about the fascinating world of DYADS. May I suggest a tome to study for yourself and friends.
The Chord Factory by Jon Damian.

Jim: Got it. B Natural Books has it. I will set up a lecture for you with the Academy's director Maestro Mejor. Let's keep in touch.

David: Thanks for the invite, Jim-E.

Jim: My pleasure, David.

JON: David Dyad's lecture was a great success, touching on peace and equality between all chords, and introducing plans for continuing work on a formal peace plan. Hey, let's check out the MAC+DC Cartoon on the back page!

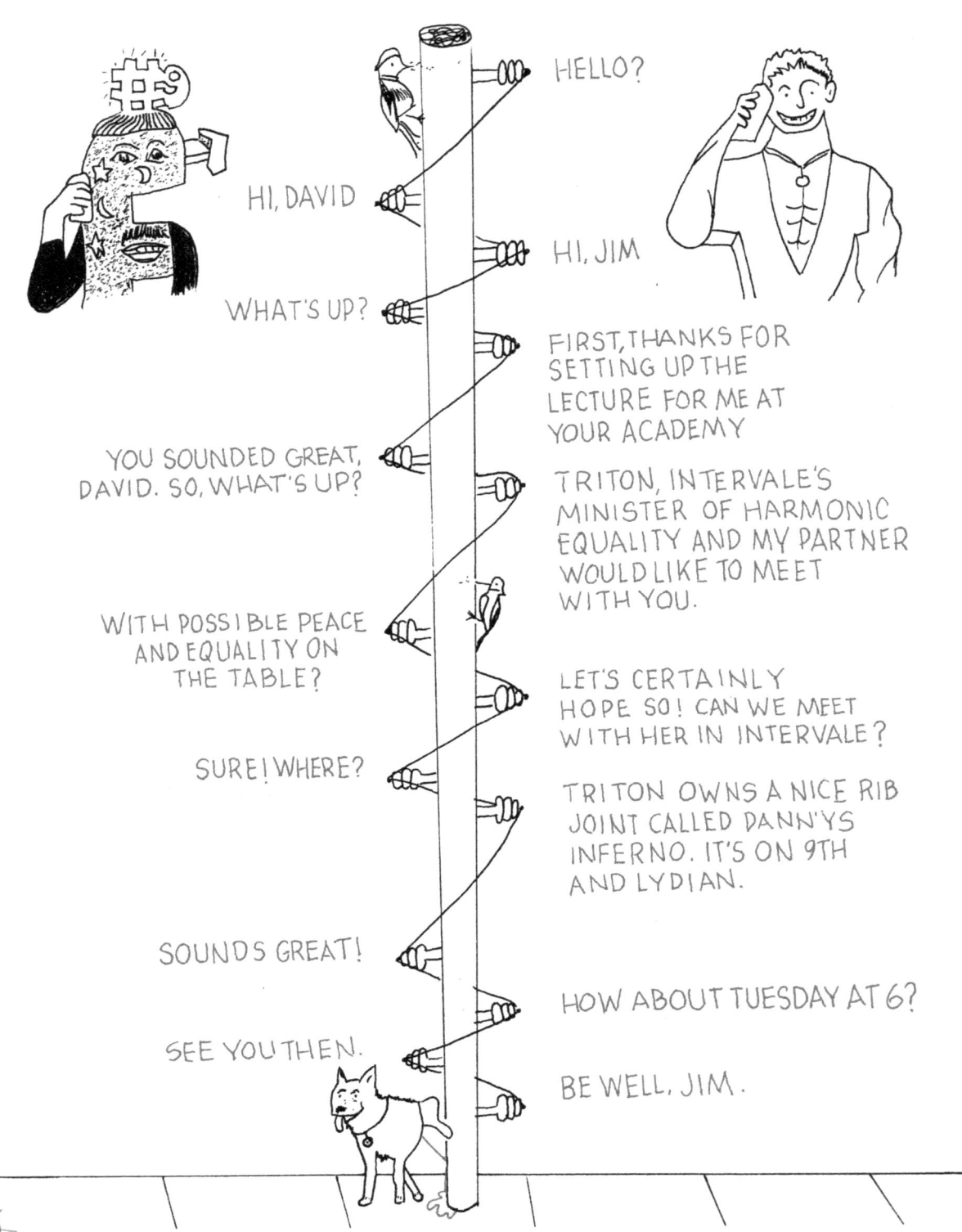

TRITON: Our Harmonyville-Intervale Peace Plan (HIPP) is in place. Hipp! Hipp! Hooray! We did it! Thanks to David and Jim.

JIM-E: It was your gracious invitation, Triton, that got things going, and David's lecture as well.

DAVID: All chords of any quality or size can now live in perfect harmony.

OBSERVER: (whispers in an English accent) Psst! She doesn't look like any Diabolus of music to me. She's lovely!

JON: This issue of the Times front page features the Harmonyville-Intervale Peace Plan meeting at Danny's Inferno in Intervale just northeast of Harmonyville. What's nice about my job as a reporter is that I get to see history being made in real time. Danny's is a great club. I got to meet David Dyad's partner Triton. My favorite item in the club is the Blues Clock, ticking along a 12-bar blues progression! Also in this issue is an article about Augie Tonale, the mayor of Augmentinia and Gino Dominante about including Augmentinia in HIPP, in memory of General Dominante, Gino's grandfather who died in the Augmentinian Conflict.

One more thing about Danny's is the incredible barbecue they serve. I have to let Bb Bobby in on their special sauce. I'll bring him some home to try. He loves to cook cajun style at his 2-5-1 Lounge and at parties and celebrations.

The Harmonyville Times

"HIPP! HIPP! THE HARMONYVILLE-INTERVALE PEACE PLAN IS IN PLACE. WE DID IT!" ANNOUNCES TRITON, INTERVALE'S MINISTER OF PEACE.

Triton, power chord David Dyad, and Harmonyville activist, Jim-E, meet at Intervale's Danny's Inferno to announce HIPP. Now all chords of any quality or size can live in perfect harmony.

In Memorium

General Dominante

David Dyad, Triton, and Jim-E

Augie Tonale, the mayor of Augmentia, Harmonyville's neighboring town to the north and Gino Dominante Harmonyville's entrepreneur and bass trombonist, met and would like to have Augmentia be a member of the HIPP plan. Tonale and Dominante also agreed that it would be a fitting memorial to Gino's grandfather, General Dominante who died in the Augmentinian conflict. David Dyad, Triton, and Jim-E agree. Mayor Tonale states, "Let us celebrate our harmonic diversity as a great gift that we can cherish. My Augmentinian heritage is based upon the whole tone producing a family rich in tritones, once thought to be the diabolo in music. Now the tritone is a valued member of our musical tradition." "I should know" Mr. Dominante says, "I am a Dominant 7 chord whose veritable heartbeat is a tritone! I have an important dominant function as a V chord and a tonic function as a I chord. I can maneuver between the two as needed." Augie and Gino have become fast friends and look forward to intertown collaborations between Augmentia and Harmonyville.

JON: Hey, this stuff is too heavy, let's check out MAC+ DC!!!

JON: Now, let's go over to Town Hall to meet Augie Tonale, a northern neighbor from Augmentinia!

Hello, citizens of Harmonyville. I am Augie Tonale, mayor of your northern neighbor, Augmentinia. Our people are harmonies from the whole-tone scale. In early times, the tritones found in this scale frightened folks who referred to them as diabolus in musica. Due to this stigma, we have suffered conflicts with other towns, including Harmonyville.

I come to thank you for embracing Augmentinia as part of HIPP! Thanks especially to Triton, David Dyad and Jim-E for drawing up the peace plan. Please visit us and enjoy our culture and friendly people. I plan to change Augmentinia's name to Holton to help clear any painful memories the town's name may conjure up. The best to all of you.

GINO: Augie, I am happy that we could finally meet thanks to the Harmonyville-Intervale Peace Plan. I appreciate your presentation. I would really like to visit Augmentinia.

AUGIE: I am honored to be invited to Harmonyville's Town Hall to speak. I would like to have you as a distinguished visitor to Augmentinia. In fact, let us make a toast in peace. I just happen to have a bottle of 100% Augmentinian Schnapps in my valise.

GINO: Good idea!

AUGIE: Na Zdraví!

GINO: Salute!

AUGIE: Say. I have a nice photo here I took at Augmentinia's annual fair last week. We have developed acrobatics and juggling into a true art form. Here is one of our acrobatic teams, Sharpie and the Sharp-Fives. Since Augmentinians are symmetrically built, all in major thirds, their natural sense of balance is uncanny!

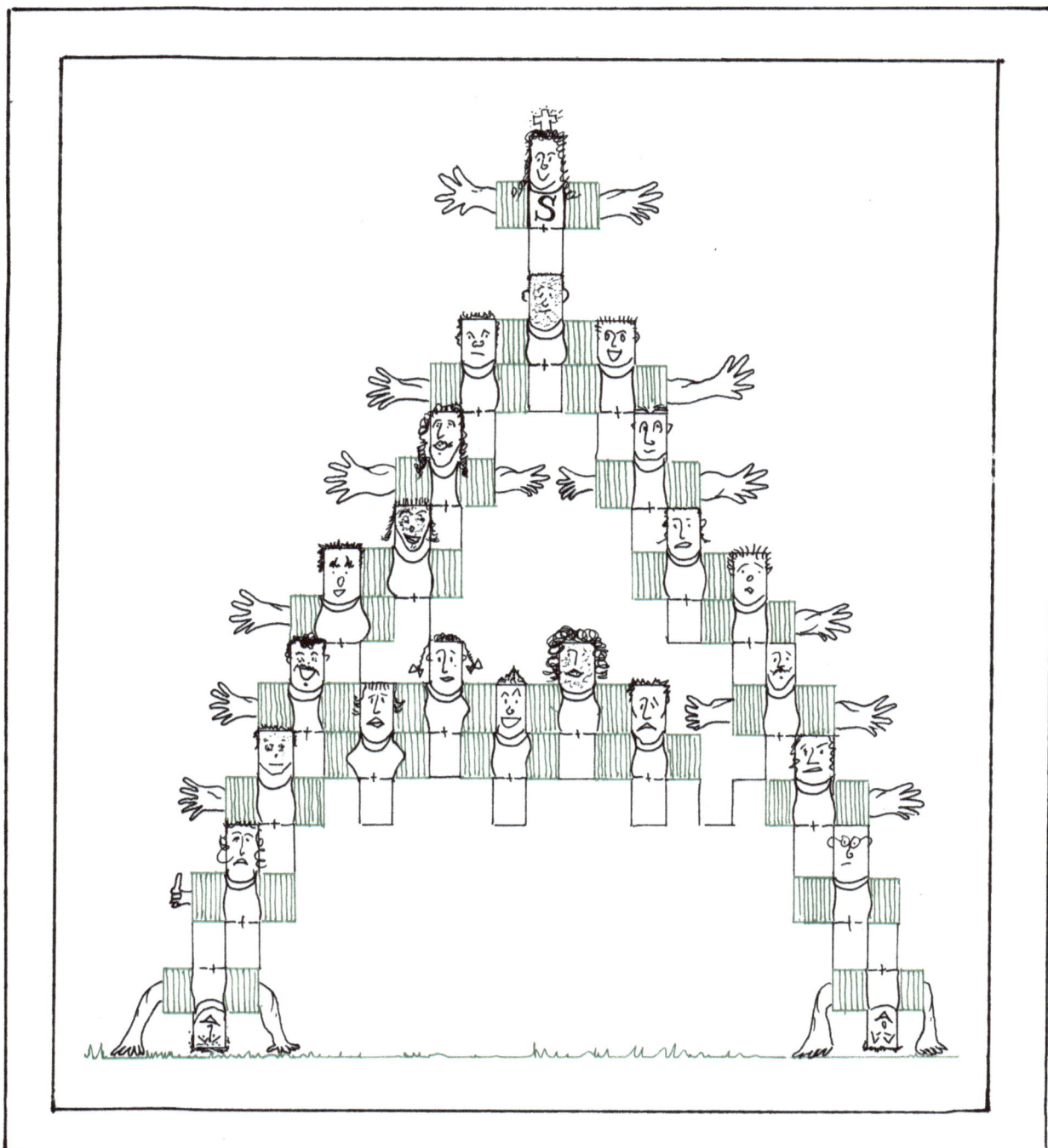

GINO: Very impressive! Thank you, Augie, for showing me that photo and for this wonderful drink. What is it called again?

AUGIE: 100% Augmentinian Schnapps!

GINO: Hey, is that my friend Jon at the end of the fourth row on the right?

AUGIE: I am not familiar with any of the troupe except for Sharpie, at the very top of the letter A. She once did forward and backward somersaults up the trail to Mt. Monad.

GINO: Wow! I've never been to Mt. Monad. I'd love to go someday.

AUGIE: The mountain is beautiful and filled with mysticism. At its peak is B Lama Monad's cave. He occasionally has visitors. One needs a special invitation to make the climb.

GINO: My dear subdominant other, Dee, speaks of B Lama often. She keeps a framed photo of him on the wall of her yoga studio.

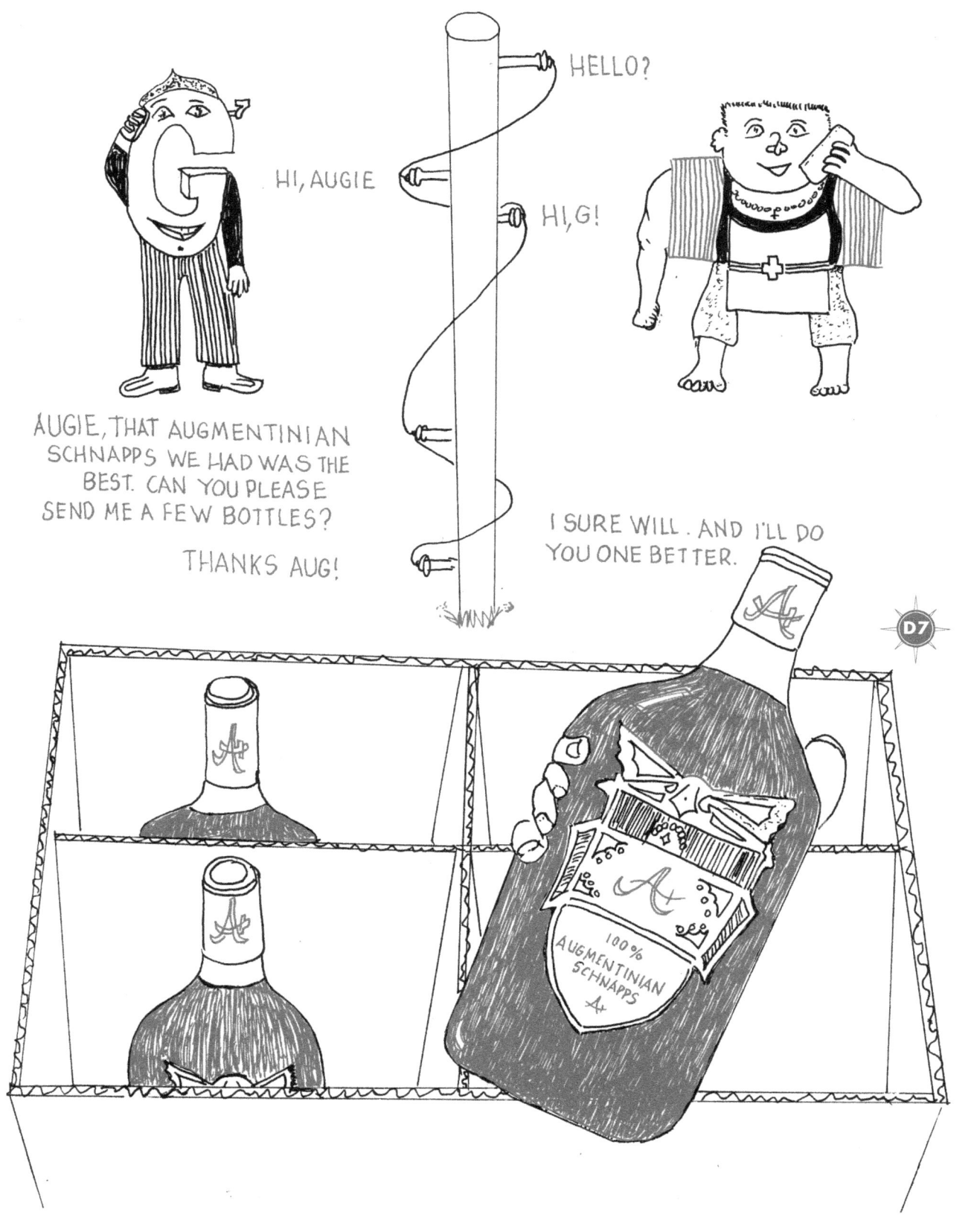

GINO: Say, Dee! I've got an ache in my belly.

DEE: Perhaps you picked up something during your road trip up north. Call Dr. Mi So. She'll check it out.

GINO: The doc says the X-ray shows I have an augmented fifth. Any ideas? It hurts!

DEE: I sure do. Let's get David Dyad, the Power Chord to guide us up to the top of Mt. Monad to see B Lama Monad. Hopefully, he can help you.

GINO: What do you know about this guy, B Lama Monad? I was recently talking to Augie about him.

DEE: From what I read in my yoga journals, he is a very special chord, consisting of just one note which gives him a spiritual stability. Sometimes the extra tension many chords take on to be cool backfires.

GINO: Wow, that makes sense. Having more is not always better. Like I've been doing with that schnapps stuff. OUCH! I like that David Dyad Power Chord guy. I know I wouldn't want to mess with him.

DEE: Oh, I wouldn't mind having a tumble with him.

GINO: Now wait a minute, Dee!?

DEE: Let's give him a buzz.

JON: Hey Bobby, just for fun let's jump into <u>The Harmonyville Times</u> WHVT chopper and check on Gino, Dee and David as they climb up Mt. Monad to confer with B Lama Monad. The mountain is only a few kilometers away. You can see it right on the horizon there. I don't mean to pry into their affairs. Being nosy is part of my job as a reporter. I'm not going to pull a paparazzi on them, I'm leaving my camera and recording equipment back at the office. I don't want to disturb B Lama Monad's meditation. I'll just circle the base of the mountain, give the folks a quick wave and then head back home.

DEE: Gino, B Lama Monad suggested meditation. I have a couple of meditation classes scheduled at my studio coming up. I know one of them you'll really like!!

GINO: That meditation stuff just puts me to sleep!

DEE: Meditation will help increase your focus and improve your health and your playing as well. And your playing could use som……

GINO: Now hold it! You try blowing into a bass trombone with a bellyache!

DEE: How can a trombone have a bellyache?

GINO: I've got the bellyache, silly!

DEE: Just joking with you, sweetie.

GINO: I love you, Dee. And I will come to study meditation with you.

DEE: You will be happy you did.

GINO: <u>OMMMM!!</u>

WELCOME TO MEDITATION 101. IN MEDITATION, A CENTRAL FOCAL POINT LIKE ONE'S BREATHING, REPETITION OF A MANTRA OR A VISUAL AID LIKE A CANDLE CAN BE HELPFUL. I RECENTLY VISITED B LAMA MONAD AT THE TOP OF MT. MONAD WITH GINO, MY SIGNIFICANT DOMINANT CHORD. DAVID DYAD WAS OUR GUIDE. B LAMA'S CHANT IS SO POWERFUL THAT HEARING IT CAN CURE ONE'S ILLS. GINO'S AUGMENTED FIFTH HAS IMPROVED THANKS TO B LAMA. HERE IS A CHANT I OFFER. I USED HARMONYVILLE'S ZIP CODE TO INSPIRE THE ACCOMPANIMENT. I HOPE IT HELPS YOUR MEDITATION. OM......

Meditation Chant

And now I'm breathing in and now I'm breathing out and

Good morning. My name is Dee, and welcome to my studio. Today, in our Meditation 102 class, we will be using a mandala. I have a new friend, Pepe Roni, who cooks at The Leaning Tower of Pizza on Bb Street. He makes a special mandala pizza. Yummm...here it is...Let's meditate on it for 20 minutes, then mangiamo!! That's "let's eat!" in Italian.

JON: Unfortunately, the meditation classes didn't help Gino. So on Dee's advice he's going to the doctor for a physical. It's no wonder his belly still aches, he ate most of that mandala pizza at the Meditation 102 class! Did you see those anchovy and hot peppers and pepperoni on that pie?! And the nice, ripe olives, swimming in the beautiful mozzarella cheese. Pepe from the Leaning Tower made that pie! He's a paisano! And an artist! In fact, rumor says that he painted the portrait of Guido Dominante that hangs in the Museum of History. He is very humble about his work. He also makes a Jackson Pollock pie that's pretty scary!! The Leaning Tower always has a line coming out the door. Get there early!!

Another benefit of being a reporter is that I can go to restaurants and eat for free if I show them my <u>Harmonyville Times</u> ID. Hey, I'm putting on weight in this town!!!

JON: Take note in Gino's medical record of his height and weight! And he is considered to be a tall chord amongst his fellow Harmies!! He's pretty wide also! His girth gives him a nice foundation for blowing his bass trombone!

The doctor also told Gino he has to go to a gym. Gino was shocked and said, "Who me? I ain't got that kinda change! I have Jon's <u>A Gym in a Sack</u> which gives plenty of exercise!! Curling with his pet rocks, Lefty and Righty, gives an upper-body workout!"

It seems that Dee is really getting fed up with Gino's weight. Especially after seeing Gino's numbers at his physical.

DEE: Gino. Give Yoga another try! I love all of you but I want your ALL to be healthy.

GINO: OK, Dee I'll try harder this time.

DEE: Your Mama C's meatballs are not helping either.

GINO: That'll kill me if I can't have my mom's lasagna and mini-meatballs!

DEE: Tell her to use chopped turkey to make her meatballs.

GINO: That would be blasphemy for her to use turkey to make her Polpette with.

DEE: Her what?

GINO: Polpette is Italian for meat-a-balls!

DEE: Oh, you are too funny, my Gino. I know everything will work out for the best. Don't tell her I suggested using turkey in her masterpiece. That would be like telling Da Vinci to use crayons on his Last Supper!

GINO: Dee Mineur is getting to be a pretty expensive sub-dominant other. I feel that it's time for a romance change!

JON: I hope that Dee didn't see him and Affy together!

Her yoga studio is right across the street!

GINO: Hey, Bobby. I got some heavy blues. Dee's done left me!

Bb BOBBY: Dr. La, the Psychordiatrist on Fifth Street is the cat for you! His office is right next to the yoga studio.

GINO: Thanks, Bobby. Dee's been spying on me, hopefully she misses me a bit. I sure miss her.

Bb BOBBY: I'm sure she does. You're a lot to miss!

GINO: Jeez, Bobby! Even you are getting down on my weight!

Bb BOBBY: I'm just trying to help you chill a bit. I've never seen you like this before.

GINO: Where's that shrink again?

Bb BOBBY: He's on Fifth Street, Dr. La is his name. I've gone to him a few times for some "adjustments."

GINO: Thanks, brother. Say, isn't Dr. La Dee's uncle?

Bb BOBBY: I believe he is. Don't worry. He's got a good reputation for helping folks. He specializes in working with artists.

DOCTOR L A HAUPT
PSYCHORDIATRIST
TENSIONS ADJUSTED

DEE: So, here's where Gino's been going! Just a tiny peek!...

DOCTOR LA HAUPT
PSYCHORDIATRIST
363 FIFTH ST. HARMONYVILLE 01625
101-625-7147

Date: 5/18/20

GINO DOMINANTE 426 D St. HARMONYVILLE 01625 6/20/80

℞ Vitamin B6 100mg cap bid

Chordazone 20mg gtt. ad lib

Aminortal 1mg tab hs.

Read: Modulating Made Easy
by Dr. James La Haupt BS.

James La Haupt

I HOPE ALL THESE MEDS CURE MY BLUES!

JON: Gino picks up his meds, and heads to the bookstore for more help.

JON: Sorry for dropping the name of one of my books, <u>The Chord Factory</u>, into the story line! Hey. It's a business?

Dearest Dee Minèur,

I saw your uncle Dr. La a few days ago and he suggested that I write you a letter of apology for my rude behavior and infidelity. I made it clear to Affy that you are my only true love. Please allow me another chance. I would love to see you soon and come to a resolution.

With all my love, your hopefully significant dominant, Gino

SAINT MONK CHORDEDRAL

Gino Baldo Dominante

&

Dee Mineur Septiéme

Happily invite you to their wedding on June 7, 2020 at 11 AM.

Service is at St. Monk Chordedral
1000 Cycle Five Drive
Harmonyville

Reception to follow at
THE CLUB
Highway 10 and Club Drive
Harmonyville.

WHAT A SWINGIN' CADENCE THEY MAKE. SHAKE RATTLE AND ROLL!!

GINO: Did you notice at the wedding the stained glass behind Reverend A Sharpe was a cycle V chart?! You have to look closely.

DEE: Yes, I did notice! It was so beautiful! So, sweetheart, now we have to plan our Harmonymoon.

GINO: How about going to a National Park?

DEE: Can't we go somewhere romantic, like Niagara Falls?

GINO: NI-A-GARA FALLS!!……NI-A-GARA FALLS!!…..INCH BY INCH……You gotta be nuts to suggest "Niagara Falls." Did you ever see that old gag? Brutal. Great slapstick though.

DEE: How about Venice?

GINO: Venice?! Why that place is sinking faster than a lead balloon! I've heard that Big Bend National Park has the most beautiful sunsets!!

DEE: OK. I'll be happy going anywhere with you, sweetie.

GINO: Likewise, Dee. I am so happy we are getting along so well.

DEE: I am, too.

GINO: Hey, let's not jinx ourselves!!

DEE: Not a chance!

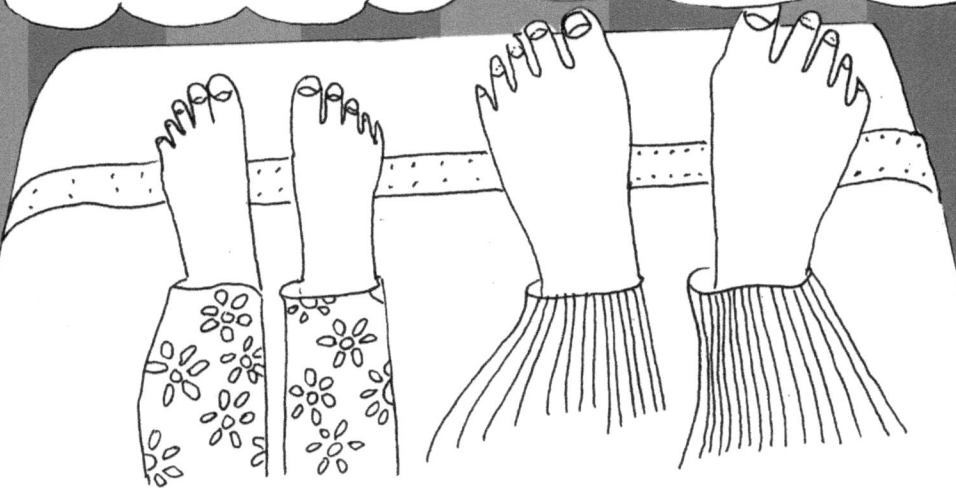

DEE: Gino, this will be my first time flying. I am quite excited. I also heard that airline food can be challenging!

GINO: I heard that also. That's why I'm packing some of Mama C's meatballs!!

DEE: Gino, be careful about getting those meatballs past security. There is a weight limitation.

GINO: No need to let me know about heavy meatballs! As a kid I developed Polpette elbow from trying to pop those suckers in whole! I had to cut them in half for my therapy to take down the inflammation.

DEE: It looks like that's not an issue for you anymore. Mama C's meatballs disappeared pretty fast at last night's going away dinner.

GINO: My mom's an artist with food. And her whistling, while she cooks, not only Neapolitan tunes but also excerpts from arias by Verdi, and Puccini. My young ears basked in the love in her whistling. Madonna Mia!!!

DEE: She's a regular prima donna!

GINO: In the best sense of the word. She is a sweetheart.

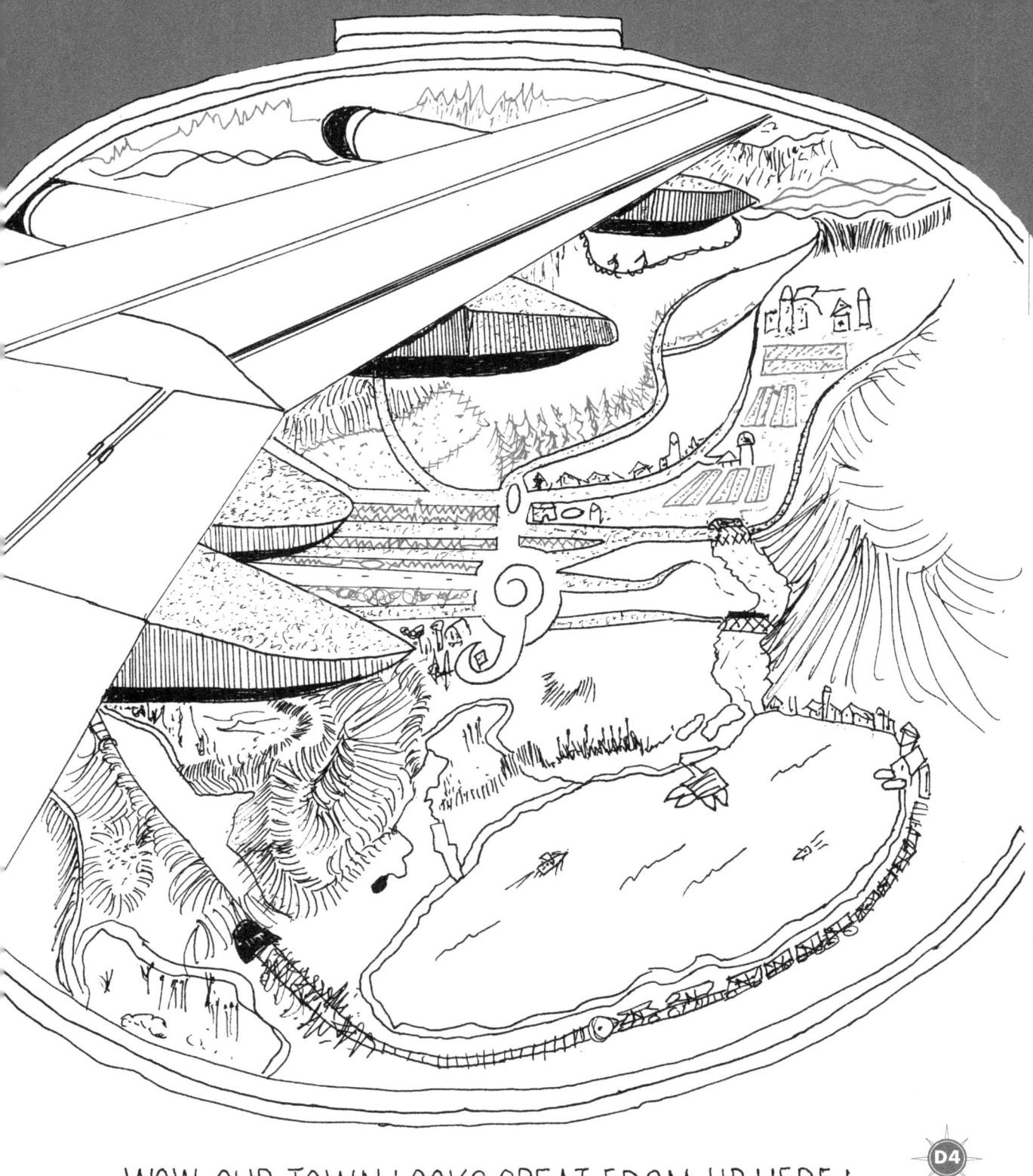

DEE: Gino, it is so beautiful flying through the clouds.

GINO: Hey! That cloud looks like a meatball! I can't believe security took my meatballs!

DEE: Gino, you'll be OK.

GINO: Even your big brown eyes look-a-like-a meatballs!

DEE: Gino, try closing your eyes and imagine counting sheep jumping over a fence.

GINO: I tried that, all I could see was meatballs jumping over a plate of ziti!!

DEE: Gino, it sounds like you will have to go to MA meetings when we get back.

GINO: What's a MA meeting?

DEE: MEATBALLS ANONYMOUS, silly!!!

GINO: HAAA!!!

DEE: So, when will you tell me where we're going?

GINO: It's a surprise. Be patient, you'll love it.

JON: I'd like to share some great news! Gino and Dee are having a baby!

THE DOMINANTE FAMILY
PAPA GINO, MAMA DEE & BABY CADENZA

JON: Can you spot Gino's second favorite drink?

GINO: I wonder what the future holds for our sweet Baby Cadenza?

DEE: Let's make an appointment with XYLA, the town mystic. She has a crystal ball and can see into the future! Have you ever seen her sculpture in the Museum of History showing a scene of harmonic evolution?

GINO: So XYLA can see into the past also?

DEE: Yep. She can.

GINO: Let's go!!

BABY CADENZA: Mama, why is that house saying hello to us?

DEE: Baby, that's XYLA'S Salon. She's going to show us her crystal ball today.

JON: It's not far from the Dominante Compound to XYLA's Parlor. She's just off Fifth Street and Bb Drive. Gino and family have arrived.

DEE: Good morning, XYLA.

XYLA: Good morning, my dears. What can I help you with?

GINO: XYLA, we would like to have some idea of what the future holds for our sweet Baby Cadenza.

XYLA: And sweet she sure is. Cootchy-coo.

BABY CADENZA: Gobble-de-goop!

XYLA: OK. Now when I begin to deliver the homily into my crystal ball, please stand back behind the curtain, you can see the ball through the peep holes. I wouldn't want you to get caught in a time warp.

DEE: What's a time warp?

XYLA: It's something like what astronomers call a black hole. Like getting caught in a vacuum.

GINO: Ouch! It's bad enough getting caught behind a vacuum!!

XYLA: It's not that, Gino. This is a lot deeper than that. Sometimes a vortex might form!

GINO: Hey, I'm leavin'!!

XYLA: Sorry to frighten you. No worries!! Let me try a future look. Here we go!!!!!

JON: Harmonyville's fortune teller, XYLA, an X Major Chord, conjures up an image from her crystal ball of the town's future. Quite amazing!

XYLA: Wow, that's amazing! My crystal ball is sure acting strange. The 23rd century!!

XYLA: Let me try backing up a bit. Here's another try!

Whooops! Now the 16th century?!!

HARMONY~VILLE IN THE 16TH CENTURY

'WHEREFORE ART THOU MY D DOMINETH SEVENETH?'

XYLA: One more try. OK! Here's a bit of the future. My ball says this is tomorrow. I forgot, it's Harmonyville's 150th birthday tomorrow! Wow! Right now, we are looking at the town's new flag being raised

GINO: Hey, Dee. There you are. I guess we're going to South Park tomorrow!

XYLA: Folks, that's the best I can do. This crystal ball needs a tune-up!! Let's try again in a week. Bye Cadenza, you baby doll.

BABY CADENZA: Ba-ba-Zee-Zee!

JON: So, Gino and his family had a nice next day at South Park. Later in the week, XYLA had some bad luck. Somehow she became trapped inside her crystal ball during a session. She may have ended up in an alternate universe. Perhaps an alternate Harmonyville, far far away?

BABY CADENZA: Da-Da G. where did Zee-Zee go?

GINO: No one knows, baby. Don't worry she's safe. Have a good sleep.

BABY CADENZA: Tank-oo Da-Da G. Mama sing Boo Moo to me?

DEE: Why sure, baby. A nice song with our town's ZIP Code in action!

BABY CADENZA: Mama, what's a zeb co??

DEE: You are too funny, babe.

DEE: Boy, what a nice guy Jon is.

GINO: Yep. He's a full-fledged Harmie now.

BABY CADENZA: Ba-ba. Ja-ja.

JON: So, dear readers, I had fun as a reporter and cartoonist for The Harmonyville Times. I regrettably have to head back home to start another cartoon project. So for now, as I drive off, I will take many sweet memories of Harmonyville with me. I hope you will also.

By the way, Gino and his family lived happily ever after.

EPILOGUE

JON: It's nice to be home. I met some nice folks in Harmonyville; especially Dee and her family. Wow, I have a nice pile of mail to check out. Why here's one from Harmonyville! It's a Dear Jon letter!!

Dear Jon,

We miss you already! Especially your MAC+DC cartoon in The Times that gave us a giggle each day. Even Baby Cadenza loves them. I caught her eating one the other day!! Would it be possible for you to send us more of your work??

Gino, Dee and Baby Cadenza.

JON: How sweet! I know just the series they would enjoy since they are animal lovers, especially Cadenza! I'll send these right off!

THREE DAYS LATER……….
BACK IN HARMONYVILLE.

DEE: Hey, Gino, here's a package from Jon! Let's take a look.

GINO: Wow, these cartoons are a hoot! Take a look. So special, since we are each other's significant other!

DEE: Who are these characters? Is that first one Jimi? Then Ella? Fun stuff.

GINO: KA-CHING!

GINO: HOLY COW(S)!!

A SMIDGE MORE!

JON: I hope Gino and Dee are enjoying the Significant series I sent them. I hope they will like to see more. It's fun sharing cartoons with folks. That's what keeps me going. In fact, I plan to use this series in my next book project "More Cartoons and Fun Stories."

Say, I just found some of my really early MAC+DC cartoons. I'll mail them right off to Dee, my biggest fan!

See you next time!
Jon

EPILOGUE PLUS

GINO eventually became mayor of Harmonyville.

DEE MINEUR SEPTIÉME changed her name to **GURU-DEE** and founded an ashram at the base of Mt. Monad, Harmonyville sector.

JON started a new cartoon series called "Birds Live." Here are his first tries....

JON: Here's a fun coincidence. Amongst the foremost "residents" at Mount Auburn Cemetery is Buckminster Fuller who invented the term geodesic dome one of which is Harmonyville's Glossarium! Here is "Bucky's" actual grave stone.

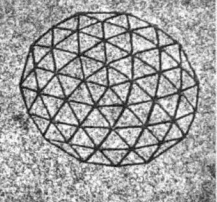

Something hit me very hard once, thinking about what one little man could do. Think of the Queen Mary—the whole ship goes by and then comes the rudder. And there's a tiny thing at the edge of the rudder called a trim tab.

It's a miniature rudder. Just moving the little trim tab builds a low pressure that pulls the rudder around. It takes almost no effort at all. So I said that the little individual can be a trim tab.
Society thinks it's going right by you, that it's left you altogether. But if you're doing dynamic things mentally, the fact is that you can just put your foot out like that and the whole big ship of state is going to go.

So I said, call me Trim Tab.

—Buckminster Fuller

PUZZLE ANSWERS

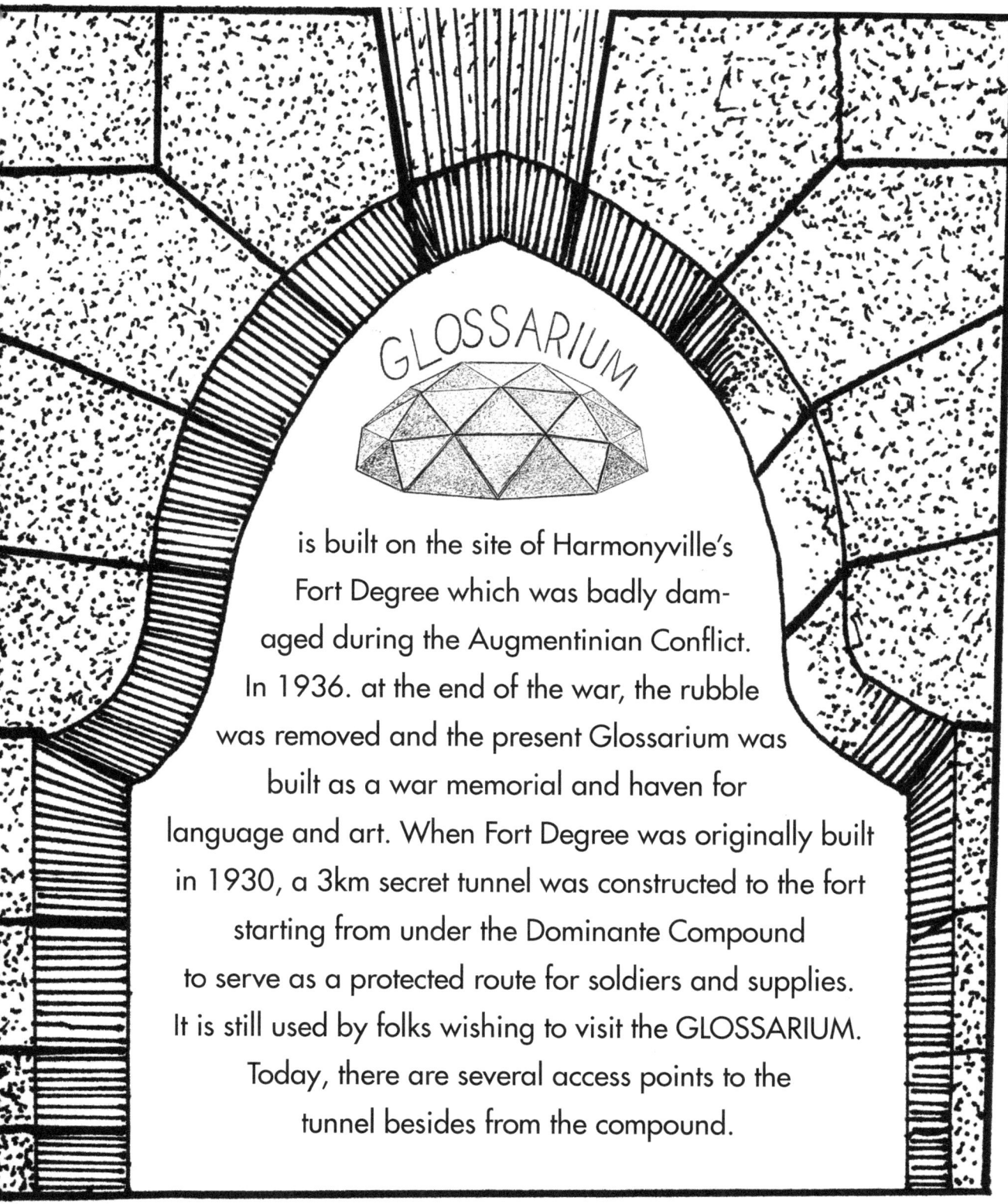

GLOSSARIUM is built on the site of Harmonyville's Fort Degree which was badly damaged during the Augmentinian Conflict. In 1936. at the end of the war, the rubble was removed and the present Glossarium was built as a war memorial and haven for language and art. When Fort Degree was originally built in 1930, a 3km secret tunnel was constructed to the fort starting from under the Dominante Compound to serve as a protected route for soldiers and supplies. It is still used by folks wishing to visit the GLOSSARIUM. Today, there are several access points to the tunnel besides from the compound.

A CAPPELLA Singing without instrumental accompaniment. The Doo Wop bands are a good example!

ALTERED A chord with one or more chromatically adjusted tones. Jim-E is an altered chord and a very good-looking one as well!

AUGMENTED FIFTH The interval of a raised fifth degree. Dr. Mi So's X-ray diagnosis of Gino's bellyache.

AUGMENTED TRIAD A chord with a major 3rd and augmented 5th. Mayor Augie Tonale of Augmentinia is an augmented triad as well as all Augmentinians.

Bb A slang adjective for a reliable or average person. Hey, Bb Bobby Straight!

CADENCE Chords used to end a phrase. Dee Mineur and Gino Dominante make for a strong cadence. Well, most of the time.

CADENZA An impressive ending and a lovely name for a baby.

CHOPS Slang for a musician's skills.

CHORD See Harmony.

CHORD SYMBOL Letters and numbers used to notate a chord. For example, G7 A Major D Minor7.

CHROMATIC APPROACH Approaching a note by a half-step.

CYCLE V CHART A circle with 12 points showing the 12 chromatic pitches moving in perfect fifths starting at C at the top. Monk Chordedral's stained glass is a beautiful example.

DIABOLUS OF MUSIC Old term for a tritone.

D MINOR 7 A sub-dominant chord in C major. Hey! Dee Mineur is one!

DOMINANT V7 See G7.

DYAD A two-note chord. Intervale's David Dyad, a Power Chord, is one.

G CLEF is also known as treble clef and indicates the G line of the music staff. The town map uses a G Clef along with the staff lines E G B D F to create an efficient route to get around town.

G7 A dominant chord in C major. Hey! Gino's one!

HARMONY Two or more notes sounding simultaneously. Listen to that boy band.

INVERTED Turning an interval or chord upside down. Not a happy situation for Gino.

KEY The central strongest tone of a scale.

MAJOR TRIAD A chord with a major 3rd and a perfect 5th. The teacher Ms. La Mejeure is a lovely one.

MODULATION A change of key. Dr. Haupt's suggestion for a hobby for Gino to help him adjust to his romance blues.

MONAD A one-note chord. B Lama Monad.

PERFECT FIFTH See Power Chord.

POWER CHORD A dyad consisting of a perfect fifth interval used in rock and Blues.

ROOT The fundamental note of a chord. Gino's is a G.

TENSIONS Notes that extend above a chord.

TRIAD A three-note chord. Jon loved singing those with his Doo-Wop band.

TRITONE The interval of a raised fourth degree Triton from Danny's Inferno is a tritone. A good-looking one too!

X MAJOR TRIAD Xyla the town mystic is an X Major chord, a fig newton of Jon's imagination.

JON'S ART HISTORY

JON: Did you see that fat albino Meatball Rat in the Glossarium? Now Harmonyville has its own Pizza Rat! Everyone calls her Ratunda. I hope you enjoyed visiting Harmonyville. I know I enjoyed creating it. I have always loved to draw, beginning as a young child doing portraits of my family. Then two years of art school at New York City Community College in Bed-Stuy, Brooklyn, led to a stint on Madison Avenue. I was drafted into the army in May 1966. After basic training, I first worked as an illustrator for officer training battalions down south and then I was shipped off to Okinawa to draw propaganda leaflets during the Vietnam conflict. After the service, I went back to Madison Avenue for a bit, then I attended Berklee College of Music on the GI Bill ("free" money). I joined the Berklee faculty during my senior year, and continued on there to spend 45 years having a great time teaching, and traveling for the school. My art chops kicked in to help me with illustrating my three published books and again here for my fourth book, <u>Welcome to Harmonyville 01625.</u>

Here is my very first gig at The Brooklyn VA hospital! The real funny part was when I dropped the drummer's ride cymbal as we exited from the hospital and it rolled down the marble walkway!! I couldn't catch it and stop it from spinning like a humongous quarter....I still remember nurses' heads sticking out of doorways with perplexed looks on their faces!...

ACKNOWLEDGMENTS

To my wonderful wife Betsy for her love and editorial patience. To all of my children, Ben, Tara, Gene, Monique-Adelle, Izzy, Elijah, Frankie and Eliana for their love. To all my family and friends who have put up with my jokes all these years. For editorial expertise, John Voigt, Carolyn Wilkins, Jonathan Feist and Evelyn Rosenthal. For technical assistance to Susan Cooley, Dave Goodrich, Abe Gurdjal, Becky Hunt, Rob Lee, Bob Nieske, Ruthie Ristich, Ralph Rosen and Frank Smith. For taking peeks, Gary Bohan, Linda Carney, Ed Fiorenza, Jim Guttmann, Nancy Lange, Justin Meyer, Joe Mulholland, Laura Murphy, Phil Neighbors, Marietta Sbraccia, Lynne Stinson, Dave Zox. Thanks to designer Kathy Kikkert and copy editor Steve Korn. Thanks to Yuto Kanazawa for his string art as Pollock pizza ingredients. Thanks for support to the lady in the Harmonyville store in Vermont. Thanks for mandala support to Martha Stewart for her perfect-sized stoneware bowl. Special thanks to Isabel Rose, my very sweet granddaughter for her especially great suggestions about colors for the books cover!!!

ABOUT THE AUTHOR

JON DAMIAN is an active international performer, composer, lecturer, clinician and author. Jon spent 45 years as a professor at The Berklee College of Music. His varied performances have ranged from Luciano Pavarotti to Bill Frisell and from the Boston Symphony Orchestra under Seiji Ozawa to Johnny Cash with the Boston Pops under John Williams. Jon Damian has recorded in a wide range of settings including The Boston Modern Orchestra Project, The Boston Pops Orchestra under Keith Lockhart and John Williams, Bill Frisell, Bob Nieske's Wolf Soup, The Boston Symphony Orchestra under Seiji Ozawa, Collage, and for NOVA. He is the author of *The Guitarist's Guide to Composing and Improvising* and *The Chord Factory: Build Your Own Guitar Chord Dictionary* available through Berklee Press and Hal Leonard Publications and *Fresh Music: Explorations with the Creative Workshop Ensemble for Musicians, Artists, and Teachers*, published by YO! Publications.

www.ingramcontent.com/pod-product-compliance
Lightning Source LLC
Chambersburg PA
CBHW061757290426
44109CB00030B/2878